You Hired Them Now What?

34 Conversation Activities To Build Rapport & Connection With Your New Team

DARIUS BROWN

Your Conversation Coach

Copyright © 2023 by Darius Brown

All rights reserved. No part of this publication may be reproduced, distributed, or transmitted in any form or by any means, including photocopying, recording, or other electronic or mechanical methods, without the prior written permission of the publisher, except in the case of brief quotations embodied in critical reviews and certain other noncommercial uses permitted by copyright law.
"You Hired Them Now What?: 34 Conversation Activities To Build Rapport & Connection With Your New Team"

ISBN: 979-8-9884858-0-3

Published by R.E.A.P Connections LLC.
www.getyourconversationcoach.com

Dedication:

This book is dedicated to all of the courageous team leaders out there who are working hard to bring their team together despite the difficulties they are encountering.

Because of the rapid pace of today's work environment, it is essential for businesses to encourage the engagement, well-being, and connectivity of their staff members. Not only does it help them feel happier as a whole, but it also results in higher levels of productivity and profitability. However, team meetings can, all too frequently, become stale and unengaging, which can lead to a disconnect between team members and a reduction in productivity.

For that reason, a book was written. The purpose of this comprehensive guide is to help teams build stronger bonds amongst each other and reawaken the flame of motivation and inspiration that once burned brightly. This book has you covered whether you're a fresh hire, a seasoned manager, or just looking to foster team spirit.

Table of Contents

Introduction: **01**

Exploring the Financial Perspectives of Your Team Members **04**

    Activity 1: The Great Investment Hunt: Finding the Best Opportunity with $5000 05

    Activity 2: Conquering Self-Doubt: Breaking Through Barriers to Reach Your Goals 09

    Activity 3: Saving and Celebrating Success: Reflecting on Hard-Earned Purchases 13

    Activity 4: Embarrassing Purchases: Lessons Learned 16

Favorite Finds: Uncovering What Your Team Loves **20**

    Activity 5: Discovering Delicious Delights: A Team's Top Food Picks 21

    Activity 6: Roaming the World: Discovering Our Favorite Destinations 24

    Activity 7: Escape to Paradise: Reflecting on Our Best Vacation Moments 27

    Activity 8: Seasons of Joy: Discovering Our Mood Boosting Months 30

    Activity 9: The Heart of Home: Discovering What Makes Us Feel Comfortable 33

Exploring Character Development and Team Growth ... **36**

    Activity 10: Friends Who Support: Celebrating Our Cheerleaders 37

    Activity 11: Overcoming Limitations: A Journey of Empowerment....40

    Activity 12: Unleashing Our Inner Animals: Exploring Personality Traits 43

Activity 13: The Heroes of Our Childhood 46

Activity 14: Discovering Our Inner Competitor: Reflecting on Life-Changing Experiences 49

Activity 15: Life on the Silver Screen: A Journey Through Our Own Personal Movie 52

Activity 16: Forgiveness in Motion 55

Exploring The Formative Years of Your Team Members 58

Activity 17: Reflecting on Roots: Celebrating Our Hometowns 59

Activity 18: Revisiting High School 62

Activity 19: Reflecting on Our High School Selves: An Exploration of Personal Growth 65

Activity 20: First Job Lessons: A Journey of Growth and Development 68

Building Relationships: Exploring Team Perspectives on Healthy Relationships 72

Activity 21: Navigating Relationships: Lessons Learned 73

Activity 22: Partnering for Success: Identifying Key Skills 76

Activity 23: Embracing Our Strengths: Exploring the Qualities that Strengthen Relationships 79

Activity 24: Celebrating Our Strengths: Building Better Relationships 82

Exploring Team Members' Personalities: Uncovering What Makes Us Unique 86

Activity 25: Building our Best Day: A Team-Building Activity 87

Activity 26: Unleashing Our Superpowers: A Team-Building Activity 90

Activity 27: Unwinding and Recharging: Exploring our Ideal Day Off 93

Activity 28: Unleashing the Alter Ego: Unleash Your Inner Focus 96

Discovering Your Team's Drive: Navigating Life Ambitions.. 100

Activity 28: Sharing Our Triumphs: Reflecting on Personal and Professional Accomplishments...101

Activity 29: Reflecting on Our Journey: The Past and Future of Our Lives...104

Activity 30: The Ultimate Choice: Business or Fortune 107

Activity 31: Risk-Taking Rewards: A Team Building Adventure 111

Activity 32: Unleashing Personal Growth: Reflecting on the Past 5 Years...114

Activity 33: CEO for a Day: Who Would You Choose? 117

Activity 34: Revelations and Reflections: The Books That Shaped Our Lives... 120

About The Author:.. 124

Additional Resources 126

Keep In Touch! 128

Introduction:

Get ready for a game-changing book that will transform the way you build rapport and connection within your new team. In today's fast-paced corporate world, your team's success is vital. As a leader, it's your role to foster connections, boost productivity, and unlock the full potential of your team members.

I've got something special just for you - "You Hired Them Now What?: 34 Conversation Activities To Build Rapport & Connection With Your New Team." This book is a treasure trove of conversation activities that will have an immediate impact on your team dynamics. No lengthy theories or complicated strategies - just practical activities that work.

Inside these pages, you'll discover 34 handpicked conversation activities that have been proven to deliver exceptional results. From icebreakers that create a welcoming and inclusive environment to engaging discussions that foster trust and collaboration, these activities are the secret sauce to building a strong and cohesive team.

I've personally curated and fine-tuned each activity based on real-world experiences. They're easy to implement and require minimal preparation. You can jump right in and start seeing positive changes within your team.

With these conversation activities, you'll unlock the full potential of your team members, ignite their passion, and promote seamless collaboration. Building strong connections and nurturing open communication will create an environment where every team member feels valued, supported, and motivated to give their best.

So, are you ready to supercharge your team's dynamics? Let's dive into this exciting journey together. Get ready to unleash the power of conversation, strengthen relationships, and take your team to new heights of success.

Here's to your success as an exceptional leader and to the unlimited potential of your incredible team.

Cheers,

Darius Brown
Your Conversation Coach

Let's jump right into the conversational activities!

EXPLORING THE FINANCIAL PERSPECTIVES OF YOUR TEAM MEMBERS

Activity 1: The Great Investment Hunt: Finding the Best Opportunity with $5000

Engaging Question: If you stumbled upon $5000, what would you consider to be the best investment opportunity to maximize your returns and why?

Purpose of this activity:

This team building exercise is designed to encourage team members to think creatively, critically, and collaboratively by exploring investment opportunities and considering the best ways to maximize returns. It promotes financial literacy, fosters discussions about goals, values, and risk tolerance, and provides insights into each team member's perspective and approach to problem-solving. The aim of this activity is to help the team learn from each other, expand their knowledge and skills, and work together to achieve common goals.

Objectives:

- Foster creative and critical thinking among team members when exploring investment opportunities.

- Increase financial literacy and knowledge of investment options.

- Promote open discussions about goals, values, and risk tolerance.

- Enhance team members' understanding of each other's perspectives and problem-solving approaches.

- Encourage teamwork, trust, and improved communication within the team through a shared learning experience.

Instructions:

1. Ask the question: "If you stumbled upon $5000, what would you consider to be the best investment opportunity to maximize your returns and why?" (5 minutes)

2. Explain the objectives of the activity (5 minutes)

3. Divide the team into small groups of 4-5 people. (5 minutes)

4. Give each group 15 minutes to brainstorm and discuss different investment options and the reasons why they believe it would be the best choice.

5. After the discussion, have each group present their

investment idea and reasoning to the rest of the team. (15 minutes per group)

6. Encourage healthy debate and discussion, where each group can ask questions, challenge each other's ideas, and provide feedback. (15 minutes)

7. After all the presentations, have the whole team vote on the best investment option based on the presentations. (10 minutes)

8. End the activity by reflecting on what the team learned from each other and what they can apply to their personal or professional lives. (15 minutes)

Materials:

- Whiteboard or flipchart and markers to write down the investment options and reasoning presented by each group.

- Timer or stopwatch to keep track of time during the brainstorming, presentation, and debate sessions.

- Index cards or sticky notes for each group to write down their investment ideas and reasoning.

- A voting system such as paper ballots or an electronic voting tool to conduct the team vote.

- Pens or pencils for each participant to take notes or jot down their thoughts during the reflection session.

- Room with enough space to accommodate the small groups and presentation setup.

- Audio-visual equipment (optional) for the presentation session if desired.

This activity is a great way for the team to develop teamwork, communication, and critical thinking skills in a fun and educational environment. By exploring investment opportunities and considering the best ways to maximize returns, the team can gain a deeper understanding of each other and work together more effectively towards common goals.

Activity 2: Conquering Self-Doubt: Breaking Through Barriers to Reach Your Goals

Engaging Question: How did you overcome self-doubt and push past mental limitations to achieve a personal or professional goal?

Purpose of this activity:

Asking team members about their experiences with overcoming self-doubt and mental barriers can be an important aspect of team building because it allows individuals to share their personal stories and lessons learned. This type of conversation can help build trust and foster a supportive environment within the team. It can also provide valuable insights into each team member's problem-solving strategies, communication styles, and motivational drivers. Additionally, hearing about others' experiences can help team members gain a better understanding of each other and can serve as a source of inspiration and encouragement. By discussing these challenges, the team can work together to find solutions and build resilience, ultimately leading to improved teamwork and collaboration.

Objective:

- Encourage team members to reflect on their experiences with overcoming self-doubt and mental barriers in achieving a goal

- Promote vulnerability and trust among team members through sharing personal challenges and experiences

- Foster a supportive and encouraging environment where team members can learn from each other and offer advice and support

- Help team members identify and understand their limiting beliefs and strategies for overcoming them

- Enhance appreciation for the diversity of perspectives, experiences, and approaches to problem-solving within the team

Instructions:

1. Divide the team into small groups of 4-5 people (5 minutes)

2. Each team member shares a personal or professional goal and the self-doubt and mental barriers they had to overcome to achieve it (3-5 minutes per person, 15-20 minutes total)

3. Allow the group to ask questions, provide support,

and offer encouragement after each share (15-20 minutes)

4. Repeat this process until all team members have shared their stories (15-20 minutes)

5. End with a discussion of what the team learned from each other and how they can apply it to their personal or professional lives (10-15 minutes)

6. Encourage each team member to take away a new perspective, renewed motivation, and stronger sense of camaraderie with colleagues (5 minutes)

Duration: Approximately 45-60 minutes

Materials:

- A large open space or room for all participants
- Writing materials (pen and paper) for each participant
- A timer or clock
- A whiteboard or flip chart paper and markers for presentation and discussion
- Optional props related to personal or professional goals to encourage participation

This team building activity provides an opportunity for team members to share their challenges and insights, build trust, and foster a supportive environment. Through learning from each other's experiences, team members can improve their teamwork, better understand each other, and build a more resilient and cohesive team. The discussion on overcoming self-doubt and mental barriers can serve as inspiration and encouragement, leading to better collaboration and a stronger team dynamic.

Activity 3: Saving and Celebrating Success: Reflecting on Hard-Earned Purchases

Engaging Question: What was the last item you saved up for, and what made it so special to you?

Purpose of this activity:

This question helps spark a conversation about hard work, perseverance, and reward. It can provide insight into each team member's values, priorities, and goals, while also fostering a supportive and encouraging environment where individuals can share their accomplishments. Additionally, this can help build connections and understanding among team members, leading to improved teamwork and collaboration.

Objectives:

- Encourage team members to share their personal stories and experiences with saving up for a special purchase.

- Foster a supportive and encouraging environment where individuals can share their accomplishments.

- Build connections and understanding among team members.

- Provide insight into each team member's values, priorities, and goals.

- Improve teamwork and collaboration through discussion and reflection.

Instructions

1. Divide the team into smaller groups of 3-5 people and ask each team member to prepare a 2-3 minute story about the last item they saved up for and what made it so special to them. (10 minutes)

2. Have each team member share their story with their small group. (15 minutes)

3. After all team members have shared their stories, ask each small group to choose the most inspiring story and present it to the larger group. (10 minutes)

4. Encourage active listening and supportive conversation among team members as they listen to each presentation. (10 minutes)

5. End the activity by reflecting on what the team learned about each other and how they can apply

it to their personal or professional lives. Have each team member share one take-away from the activity. (10 minutes)

Duration for this activity: 60-minute session.

Materials:

➢ None, this is a discussion-based activity.

Asking team members about their experiences saving for something they were excited about can be a valuable team-building activity. It encourages team members to share their personal stories and reflect on their hard work and achievements. This type of conversation can help build relationships and foster a positive and supportive work environment. It can provide insights into each team member's money management skills, spending habits, and motivation. By discussing these experiences, the team can learn from each other, exchange ideas and tips, and ultimately grow together as a team.

Activity 4: Embarrassing Purchases: Lessons Learned

Engaging Question: What was your worst purchase ever, and what did you learn from the experience?

Purpose of this activity:

This question encourages team members to share their personal stories and experiences with money management. It can foster a supportive environment within the team and help build trust. It can also provide valuable insights into each team member's financial decision-making processes, and serve as a source of inspiration and encouragement.

Objectives:

- To promote financial literacy and encourage open discussion about money management.

- To build trust and foster a supportive environment within the team.

- To gain a better understanding of each team

member's financial decision-making processes.

- To provide a source of inspiration and encouragement.

- To learn from each other's experiences and develop better money management skills.

Instructions:

1. Divide the team into small groups of 4-5 people. (5 minutes)

2. Give each group 15 minutes to discuss their worst purchase ever and what they learned from the experience. (15 minutes)

3. Have each group present their story to the rest of the team. (10 minutes)

4. Encourage healthy debate and discussion, where each group can ask questions, challenge each other's ideas, and provide feedback. (10 minutes)

5. End the activity by reflecting on what the team learned from each other and what they can apply to their personal or professional lives. (5 minutes)

Duration: 30-45 minutes

Materials:

- Whiteboard or flip chart and markers/pens
- Timer or clock

By discussing their experiences with embarrassing purchases, the team can learn from each other and develop better money management skills. This type of conversation can help build trust and foster a supportive environment within the team, and can provide valuable insights into each team member's financial decision-making processes. It can also serve as a source of inspiration and encouragement for the team.

FAVORITE FINDS: UNCOVERING WHAT YOUR TEAM LOVES

Activity 5: Discovering Delicious Delights: A Team's Top Food Picks

Engaging Question: What are the top 3 cuisines or foods that get your taste buds dancing?

Purpose of this activity:

Discussing food preferences can be a fun and lighthearted way to bring a team together and foster camaraderie. It can also give team members an opportunity to learn about each other's cultural backgrounds and personal tastes.

Objectives:

- To foster teamwork and build rapport among team members.

- To promote cultural awareness and appreciation.

- To encourage open communication and active listening.

- To learn about each team member's food preferences and favorite cuisines.

Instructions:

1. Divide the team into small groups of 4-5 people and assign a facilitator for each group. The facilitator should keep track of time and ensure that everyone in the group has a chance to participate. (2-5 minutes)

2. Give each group 15 minutes to brainstorm and discuss their top 3 cuisines or foods and why they love them. Encourage them to think about the flavors, aromas, cultural significance, and personal experiences associated with their favorite foods. (15 minutes)

3. Have each group present their favorite cuisines and reasons to the rest of the team, taking turns and giving each other their full attention. Encourage each member of the group to participate in the presentation, either by speaking or assisting with the presentation. (5-20 minutes)

4. Encourage team members to ask questions and try new foods if they can. The goal is to learn about each other's food preferences and cultural backgrounds. (10-15 minutes)

5. End the activity by reflecting on what the team learned about each other's food preferences and cultural backgrounds. This reflection can be done through a group discussion or individually writing down what they learned. (10-15 minutes)

Duration: 30 minutes to 1 hour

Materials:

- Whiteboard or flipchart and markers for presentations
- Timekeeper (can be a smartphone or timer)
- Optional: food samples or pictures of different cuisines to enhance the presentation and discussion.

This team building activity provides a fun and interactive way for team members to get to know each other on a personal level, learn about different cultures and cuisines, and promote teamwork and open communication. It also serves as a reminder that everyone has different tastes and preferences, and that it's important to respect and appreciate each other's differences.

Activity 6: Roaming the World: Discovering Our Favorite Destinations

Engaging Question: What city have you fallen in love with and can't wait to visit again?

Purpose of this activity

Asking team members about their favorite cities and travel experiences can help build camaraderie and foster a better understanding of each other's interests and personalities. It can also provide insights into different cultures and perspectives, leading to enhanced teamwork and communication.

Objectives:

- To encourage team members to share their travel experiences and favorite destinations

- To build a sense of camaraderie and trust among team members

- To foster a better understanding of different cultures and perspectives

- To improve communication and teamwork within the team

Instructions:

1. Divide the team into small groups of 4-5 people, based on the group size, and assign a facilitator for each group. The facilitator should keep track of time and ensure that everyone in the group has a chance to participate. (2-5 minutes)

2. Give each group 10 minutes to discuss their favorite city and why they love it. Encourage them to think about the cultural attractions, local cuisine, history, climate, and personal experiences that make their favorite city special. (10 minutes)

3. Have each group present their city and reasons to the rest of the team, taking turns and giving each other their full attention. Encourage each member of the group to participate in the presentation, either by speaking or assisting with the presentation. (15-20 minutes)

4. Encourage open discussion and ask each group to share their thoughts on other cities presented. The goal is to learn about each other's travel experiences and preferences. (10-15 minutes)

5. End the activity by summarizing what the team learned about each other and how it can benefit their

work together. This reflection can be done through a group discussion or individually writing down what they learned. (10-15 minutes)

Duration: 50-60 minutes

Materials needed:

- Whiteboard or flipchart and markers for presentations
- Timekeeper (can be a smartphone or timer)
- Optional: pictures or maps of different cities to enhance the presentation and discussion.

Exploring our favorite cities can be a fun and insightful team building activity. By sharing our travel experiences and learning about each other's favorite destinations, we can build camaraderie, foster a better understanding of different cultures and perspectives, and improve communication and teamwork within the team. This activity can also provide a break from work-related discussions and help team members connect on a more personal level, leading to a more positive and supportive work environment.

Activity 7: Escape to Paradise: Reflecting on Our Best Vacation Moments

Engaging Question: What was the best part of the last vacation you took?

The purpose of this activity:

Understanding what each team member values in a vacation experience can provide insight into their interests, preferences, and priorities. This can help build a more cohesive team and create a sense of connection between team members.

Objectives:

- To understand each team member's travel preferences and interests.

- To encourage open communication and build trust within the team.

- To foster a positive and supportive team environment.

- To provide team members with an opportunity to share their experiences and connect with others.

Instructions

1. Explain the activity to the team and emphasize the importance of active listening and respectful dialogue. (2-3 minutes)

2. Have each team member take turns sharing the best part of their last vacation and why it was special to them. Encourage them to share personal experiences and feelings, as well as to be concise and concise in their presentations. (15-20 minutes)

3. Encourage team members to ask questions and engage in discussion to build a better understanding of each other's experiences. For example, they can ask follow-up questions about the destination, the activities, or the highlights of the trip. (10-15 minutes)

4. After each person has shared, reflect as a team on common themes or similarities that emerged and discuss what they mean for the team. For example, they can discuss common interests, shared experiences, or similarities in how they approach leisure time. (5-10 minutes)

Duration: 30-40 minutes

Materials:

- Whiteboard or flipchart and markers for presentations
- Timekeeper (can be a smartphone or timer)
- Optional: pictures or maps of different cities to enhance the presentation and discussion.

Sharing experiences from past vacations can bring team members closer together and deepen their understanding of each other's interests and priorities. This activity encourages open communication and builds a positive and supportive team environment. By reflecting on their experiences, team members can gain new insights and create a sense of connection that can be applied to their work together.

Activity 8: Seasons of Joy: Discovering Our Mood Boosting Months

Engaging Question: Which seasons of the year bring you the most happiness and energy? Why?

Purpose of this activity:

Understanding the seasons and times of year that bring joy and positive energy to team members can help create a more harmonious and supportive work environment. It can also provide insights into individual preferences, work styles, and motivations.

Objectives:

- To foster open and honest communication among team members

- To gain a better understanding of each team member's preferences and motivations

- To promote a positive and supportive work environment

- To encourage creativity and collaboration

- To learn about different perspectives and experiences.
- Conversational Team Building Activity: "Seasonal Reflections"

Instructions:

1. Divide the team into pairs, either randomly or by choice. (2-3 minutes)

2. Ask each pair to discuss their favorite season and why it brings them joy and energy. Encourage them to share personal experiences and feelings, as well as to be concise and concise in their discussions. (10-15 minutes)

3. After each pair has finished their discussion, ask each person to share one thing they learned about their partner's favorite season. Encourage them to be specific and highlight the differences or similarities between their favorite seasons. (5-10 minutes)

4. Repeat this process until every team member has had a chance to share. Encourage the team to ask questions and engage in discussion to build a better understanding of each other's experiences and preferences. (10-15 minutes)

5. End the activity by summarizing what the team learned about each other and how it can benefit their work together. For example, they can discuss common interests, shared experiences, or similarities

in how they approach different seasons. (5-10 minutes)

Duration: 30-45 minutes

Materials:

- Whiteboard or flipchart and markers for presentations
- Timekeeper (can be a smartphone or timer)

By learning about each other's favorite seasons and experiences, we can build stronger relationships, promote positive energy and collaboration, and create a more enjoyable and supportive work environment.

Activity 9: The Heart of Home: Discovering What Makes Us Feel Comfortable

Engaging Question: What are the three most important things in your home that make it feel like a place of comfort and security? Why are they so important to you?

Purpose of the activity:

Understanding what makes each team member feel comfortable and at home can help create a more supportive and inclusive work environment. It can also provide insights into individual preferences and help team members get to know each other on a personal level.

Objectives:

- To foster open and honest communication among team members

- To gain a better understanding of each team member's preferences and needs

- To promote a supportive and inclusive work environment

- To encourage creativity and collaboration

- To learn about different perspectives and experiences.

- Interactive Team Building Activity: "Creating a Home Away from Home"

Instructions:

1. Divide the team into small groups of 4-5 people, based on group size. (5 minutes)

2. Give each group 20 minutes to brainstorm and come up with their ideas on how to bring elements of "home" into the work environment. (20 minutes)

3. Have each group present their ideas to the rest of the team in a clear and concise manner, taking no more than 5 minutes per presentation. (15 minutes)

4. Encourage open discussion and questions after each presentation. (10 minutes)

5. Allow the team to vote on their favorite idea, using a show of hands or another agreed upon method. (5 minutes)

6. End the activity by announcing the winning group and congratulating them on their ideas. (5 minutes)

The winning group can then implement their ideas in the workplace.

Duration: 1 hour

Materials:

- Whiteboard and markers (or flip chart and markers) for each group to present their ideas
- Ballot box or other method for collecting and counting votes.

By exploring what makes us feel comfortable and at home, we can create a more supportive and inclusive work environment and build stronger relationships with our colleagues. Through this activity, we can gain a better understanding of each other's preferences and needs, encourage creativity and collaboration, and learn about different perspectives and experiences.

EXPLORING CHARACTER DEVELOPMENT AND TEAM GROWTH

Activity 10: Friends Who Support: Celebrating Our Cheerleaders

Engaging Question: How do your friends show up for you to make you feel supported? Share a few examples.

Purpose of the Activity:

Understanding how our friends support us can give us insights into what makes us feel valued and appreciated. This can also help to foster a supportive work environment where team members can rely on one another for support.

Objectives:

- To encourage open and honest communication among team members

- To gain a better understanding of each team member's support system and what makes them feel valued

- To promote a positive and supportive work environment

- To encourage teamwork and collaboration

➢ To learn about different perspectives and experiences.

Instructions

1. Divide the team into small groups of 4-5 people each (based on group size). (5 minutes)

2. Instruct each team member to share one example of how a friend has shown up for them to make them feel supported. This could be a specific instance or a general behavior that has made a difference. (10-15 minutes per group)

3. Have the groups discuss and identify common themes among the examples shared by each team member. Encourage each group to discuss why these supportive behaviors were meaningful and what impact they had. (10-15 minutes)

4. Each group can then share their findings with the rest of the team. (5-10 minutes per group)

5. Finally, as a team, discuss ways to incorporate these supportive behaviors into the work environment. This could be done through encouraging open communication, promoting a positive work culture, or finding ways to acknowledge and reward supportive behaviors. (15-20 minutes for the entire team.)

Duration: Approximately 45 minutes to 1 hour

Materials:

➢ Writing materials (pen, paper, etc.)

➢ Flip chart or whiteboard for group discussions

By exploring how our friends support us, we can gain a better understanding of what makes us feel valued and appreciated. This can help to create a more positive and supportive work environment where team members can rely on one another for support and feel valued for their contributions.

Activity 11: Overcoming Limitations: A Journey of Empowerment

Engaging Question: What limiting beliefs or insecurities have you overcome and what was your journey like?

Objectives:

- To encourage open and honest communication among team members

- To foster a supportive and non-judgmental environment

- To highlight individual strengths and resilience

- To promote collaboration and problem-solving among team members

- To inspire growth and personal development within the team

Purpose of the activity:

The purpose of this activity is to encourage team members to share their personal growth experiences and to foster a supportive and non-judgmental environment. Through reflecting on the journeys of overcoming limiting beliefs and insecurities, the activity aims to promote empathy, understanding, and trust among team members and strengthen relationships within the team. Additionally, by sharing stories of resilience and personal growth, the activity may inspire others to overcome their own challenges and foster a positive team dynamic.

Instruction:

1. Divide the team into small groups of 4-5 members each (5 minutes)

2. Give each group a set of prompts to start the conversation (30-40 minutes per group):

    a. Prompts could include "What limiting beliefs or insecurities have you overcome?" or "What was your journey like?"

    b. Encourage each group member to actively listen and empathize with others in their group.

3. Have each group present their story to the rest of the team (10-15 minutes per group):

    a. Encourage open and respectful discussion among the team members and ask questions for further understanding.

4. Have the team come together to brainstorm

ways they can support each other in overcoming challenges in the future (20-30 minutes for the entire team):

   a. Use the whiteboard and markers or a large paper and pens to document their ideas.

5. Wrap up the activity: Summarize the main takeaways and action items from the discussion. (5-10 minutes)

Materials:

- Whiteboard or flipchart
- Markers or pens
- Prompts or questions for each group to start the conversation
- Timekeeper (to ensure the activity stays on track and within the allotted time)

This activity aims to promote open communication, empathy, and support among team members. By sharing their experiences of overcoming limiting beliefs and insecurities, team members can gain a deeper understanding of each other and collaborate more effectively in the future. The final discussion can help the team identify specific ways they can support each other and foster a culture of growth and personal development.

Activity 12: Unleashing Our Inner Animals: Exploring Personality Traits

Engaging question: Which animal traits do you see in yourself and why?

Why this question is important: Understanding our personality traits can help us understand our strengths and weaknesses, and how we can work better with others. By relating ourselves to animals, we can have a fun and lighthearted way to approach the topic.

Objectives:

- To help team members understand their personality traits and strengths.

- To encourage team members to share and learn about each other in a fun and lighthearted way.

- To foster open communication and build stronger relationships within the team.

- To promote self-awareness and reflection on personal traits.

- To explore different perspectives and ways of approaching challenges and tasks.

Instructions:

1. Divide the team into small groups of 4-5 members (5 minutes)

2. Provide each group with paper, pens, and markers (5 minutes)

3. Ask each member to take a few minutes to think about the animal traits they relate to and why (10 minutes)

4. Ask each member to draw a picture of the animal they have chosen and write a brief explanation of why they have chosen that animal (10 minutes)

5. Once each member has completed their picture and explanation, have each group share their drawings and explanations with the rest of the team (10 minutes per group)

6. Encourage open discussion and collaboration within each group and with the whole team (10-15 minutes)

7. Have the team brainstorm ways they can support each other and work together better based on their animal traits (15-20 minutes)

Duration: 1 hour

Materials:

- Paper
- Pens
- Markers

This activity is a fun and engaging way to encourage team members to explore their personality traits and better understand themselves and each other. By sharing and discussing their chosen animal traits, the team can build stronger relationships and work together more effectively in the future.

Activity 13: The Heroes of Our Childhood

Engaging Question: Who were some of the people you looked up to or wanted to be like growing up and why?

Purpose of this activity:

This question can help team members reflect on their personal and cultural influences, as well as their values and aspirations. It can also lead to discussions about how those influences have shaped their current perspectives and goals.

Objectives:

- To reflect on personal and cultural influences

- To understand team members' values and aspirations

- To facilitate discussion and collaboration among team members

- To increase empathy and understanding within the team

- To encourage personal and professional growth through sharing experiences

Instructions:

1. Divide the team into small groups of 4-6 people: 5 minutes

2. Reflect on the question: "Who were some of the people you looked up to or wanted to be like growing up and why?": 5 minutes per person

3. Share answer with the group: 10-15 minutes per person

4. Group discussion and collaboration: 15-20 minutes per group

5. Share insights and experiences with the rest of the team: 5-10 minutes per group

6. Larger group discussion around the theme of influences, values, and aspirations: 20-30 minutes for the entire team

7. Wrap up the activity: 5 minutes

Time Duration: 45 minutes to 1 hour

Materials Needed:

- A large room or open space for the groups to gather
- A timer or clock to keep track of time
- Whiteboard or flip chart to capture key insights and discussion points

This activity helps team members reflect on their personal and cultural influences, values, and aspirations. It provides an opportunity for team members to learn from each other and gain a better understanding of each other's backgrounds, experiences, and perspectives. By sharing stories and discussing the impact of our heroes and role models, the team can increase empathy, foster collaboration, and support personal and professional growth.

Activity 14: Discovering Our Inner Competitor: Reflecting on Life-Changing Experiences

Engaging Question: What competitive environments have you been in that taught you the most about yourself or life?

Purpose of the activity:

Understanding our experiences in competitive environments can provide insight into our strengths, weaknesses, values, and how we handle stress and pressure. By reflecting on these experiences, we can learn more about ourselves and each other, and use that knowledge to improve our teamwork and communication.

Objectives:

- To reflect on personal experiences in competitive environments
- To understand how these experiences have shaped the way we approach challenges and handle stress

- To learn about our colleagues' experiences and perspectives

- To improve communication and empathy within the team

- To identify ways to support each other in future challenges and stressful situations

Instructions:

1. Pose the engaging question to the whole team.

2. Explain the purpose & objectives of the activity

3. Divide the team into small groups of 3-4 people (5 minutes).

4. Give each group a set of questions to guide their discussion, such as:

   a. What was the competitive environment you were in? (5 minutes)

   b. What did you learn about yourself or life through that experience? (10 minutes)

   c. What were some of the challenges you faced and how did you overcome them? (10 minutes)

   d. How do you think that experience has shaped the way you approach challenges or handle stress now? (10 minutes)

5. Allow each group 20-30 minutes to discuss their experiences and answers to the questions.

6. Have each group present their findings to the rest of the team, encouraging discussion and collaboration (15-20 minutes).

7. End the activity by asking the team to brainstorm ways they can support each other in future challenges and stressful situations (15-20 minutes).

Time Duration: 1 hour

Materials Needed:

- A set of guiding questions for each group
- Writing materials for each participant to take notes
- A whiteboard or flipchart for each group to present their findings

This activity encourages participants to reflect on their experiences in competitive environments and how they have shaped their approach to challenges and handling stress. By learning about each other's experiences, the team can improve communication, empathy, and support for each other in future challenges.

Activity 15: Life on the Silver Screen: A Journey Through Our Own Personal Movie

Engaging Question: If a movie was made about your life right now, what would be the title and which person would have made the most appearances?

Purpose of the Activity: Understanding each team member's experiences, perspectives and relationships can help build stronger connections and empathy within the team. By sharing stories and experiences, team members can get to know each other on a deeper level, leading to better collaboration and communication.

Objectives:

- To foster a deeper understanding of each team member's experiences and perspectives.

- To encourage open and effective communication within the team.

- To build empathy and strengthen connections among team members.

- To provide a fun and engaging way for team members

to get to know each other.

- To stimulate creativity and encourage team members to think outside the box.

Instructions:

1. Divide the team into small groups of 3-5 people. (5 minutes)

2. Give each person 5-7 minutes to share their story, answering the question posed. (35-45 minutes)

3. After each person has shared, allow time for the rest of the group to ask questions and provide feedback. (10-15 minutes)

4. After each small group has finished, have each group present their stories to the larger team. (15-20 minutes)

5. Encourage open and respectful discussion among the team members. (15-20 minutes)

Duration: 45 minutes to 1 hour and 30 mins.

Materials: None, just a space for the team to gather and speak.

This activity provided a fun and engaging way for team members to get to know each other on a deeper level, building stronger connections and empathy within the team. By sharing stories and experiences, team members were able to better understand each other's perspectives and experiences, leading to more effective collaboration and communication in the future.

Activity 16: Forgiveness in Motion

Engaging Question: Have you ever had to forgive someone for something? How did you handle the situation?

Purpose of this activity:

Forgiveness is an important aspect of human relationships, both personal and professional. Team building meetings provide a platform for team members to learn and grow from each other's experiences, and discussing forgiveness can help team members understand each other's perspectives and foster a more positive and supportive work environment.

Objectives:

- To encourage team members to reflect on their past experiences with forgiveness.

- To provide a safe and supportive environment for team members to share their stories.

- To foster empathy and understanding among team members.

- To promote a positive and supportive work environment through open communication and collaboration.

- To learn from each other's experiences and incorporate new insights into their personal and professional lives.

Instructions:

1. Divide the team into small groups of 3-5 people.

2. Give each group a prompt card that asks "When was the last time you had to forgive someone for something? How did that situation turn out?"

3. Allow each group 10-15 minutes to discuss their experiences with forgiveness and share their stories with each other.

4. Once all groups have finished, ask each group to present their story to the rest of the team.

5. Encourage team members to ask questions and provide support for each other.

6. Allow 20-30 minutes for the team to discuss forgiveness and its impact on relationships.

7. Wrap up the activity with a summary of the key takeaways and any next steps for continued

growth and development in this area for team building.

Time Duration: 30-45 minutes

Materials:

- Prompt cards (1 per group)
- Writing materials (e.g. paper, pens)
- Timer

The activity helped team members reflect on their past experiences with forgiveness. Team members were able to share their stories and learn from each other's experiences. The activity fostered empathy and understanding among team members, promoting a positive and supportive work environment.

EXPLORING THE **FORMATIVE** YEARS OF YOUR TEAM MEMBERS

Activity 17: Reflecting on Roots: Celebrating Our Hometowns

Engaging Question: What are the three most memorable aspects of the place where you grew up?

Purpose of this activity:

This question is important in team building meetings as it helps team members understand each other's background and experiences. It also helps to create a sense of belonging and foster a positive team culture.

Objectives:

- To encourage team members to reflect on their hometowns and childhood experiences.

- To provide a platform for team members to share and learn about each other's hometowns.

- To build team rapport and encourage positive team culture.

- To foster team members' sense of belonging and create a more inclusive environment.

- To help team members understand and appreciate the diversity of their backgrounds and experiences.

Instructions:

1. Divide the team into small groups of 4-5 people (0-5 minutes)

2. Each team member should take 5-7 minutes to reflect on their hometown and write down three things they love about it (5-7 minutes)

3. Challenge each team member to pull out their phone to find a picture of one of their hometown favorites on Google Maps and share it with the rest of the team (10-15 minutes)

   a. This can be a landmark, a local business, a natural wonder, or anything else that represents the essence of their hometown.

   b. Encourage everyone to ask questions about each picture and discuss what makes each hometown special

4. Bring the whole team together and ask each small group to share one or two things they learned about their teammate's hometown (5-10 minutes for presentation).

5. End the challenge by thanking everyone for participating and for sharing a little piece of their hometown with the rest of the team (1-2 minutes).

Duration: 45 - 60 minutes

Materials:

➢ Writing paper and pens or markers for each team member

This activity provides an opportunity for team members to reflect on their hometowns and childhood experiences, which can help to build team rapport and foster a positive team culture. By encouraging team members to share and learn about each other's hometowns, the activity helps to foster a sense of belonging and create a more inclusive environment.

Activity 18: Revisiting High School

Engaging Question: What two things do you wish you had learned more about during your high school years?

Purpose of this activity:

By reflecting on their high school experiences, team members can identify areas of interest or passion they may have overlooked in the past. This can help to build a better understanding of each other's strengths, values, and goals. Additionally, discussing what they wish they had learned more about can lead to new ideas and learning opportunities for the team.

Objectives:

- To encourage team members to reflect on their high school experiences
- To build a deeper understanding of each other's values, interests, and goals
- To identify areas for personal and professional growth

- To foster communication and collaboration among team members

- To encourage team members to continue learning and growing in their careers.

Instructions:

1. Divide the team into small groups of 4-5 people. (5 minutes)

2. Give each group a flip chart and markers. (2 Mins)

3. Ask each team member to write down 2 things they wish they had learned more about during high school. (5 Mins)

4. Once everyone has written down their answers, ask each team member to take turns sharing their answers with the group and why they chose those subject matters. (10 Mins)

5. Once everyone has had a chance to share, ask each team to come up with 2-3 actionable steps they can take to continue learning and growing in the areas they wish they had learned more about. Give each team 5-10 minutes to discuss and come up with their action plan. (5-10 mins)

6. After the time is up, ask each team to present their action plan to the rest of the team. (15 Mins)

a. Encourage the rest of the team to ask questions, offer suggestions, and give support.

Time Duration: 45-60 minutes

Materials: flipcharts, pens, markers

By reflecting on their high school experiences and what they wish they had learned more about, team members were able to build a deeper understanding of each other's values, interests, and goals. They also identified areas for personal and professional growth and created action plans to continue learning and growing. This activity fostered communication and collaboration among team members and encouraged them to continue pursuing their passions.

Activity 19: Reflecting on Our High School Selves: An Exploration of Personal Growth

Engaging Question: What do you think you were best known for during your high school years, and how has that changed for you now?

Purpose of this activity:

High school is a formative time in many people's lives, and reflecting on our experiences during this time can help us better understand who we are and how we have grown. Sharing these experiences with others in a team building setting can help to build stronger relationships, encourage empathy and understanding, and create a sense of connection and community within the team.

Objectives:

- To encourage self-reflection and personal growth
- To foster empathy and understanding among team members

- To promote open and honest communication within the team

- To build a sense of community and connection among team members

- To promote a positive and supportive work environment

Instructions:

1. Divide the team into small groups of 4-6 people. (10 minutes)

2. Ask each team member to write down their answer to the question on a sticky note. (5 minutes)

3. Each team member takes turns sharing their answer and sticks their note on a designated wall or board. (5 minutes per person)

4. Encourage each team member to listen actively and ask questions to show their interest and understanding. (10 minutes per person)

5. After each person has had a chance to share, encourage the group to categorize the sticky notes into common themes or patterns that emerged during the sharing. (15 minutes per group)

6. Each team presents their categorization and insights to the rest of the team. (10 minutes per group)

7. As a team, discuss any common themes or patterns that emerged during the small group discussions and reflect on how those things have changed or evolved over time. (15-30 minutes)

8. Finally, have each team member write down one action they can take to continue growing and developing in the areas they wish they had more of in high school. (5 minutes)

Duration for the Activity: 60 - 90 minutes

Materials: flip charts, sticky notes, markers, pens

This activity provides an opportunity for team members to reflect on their high school experiences and share their personal growth with each other. It promotes open and honest communication, empathy and understanding, and helps to build a sense of community and connection within the team. By sharing their experiences, team members are able to gain a deeper understanding of each other and to foster a positive and supportive work environment.

Activity 20: First Job Lessons: A Journey of Growth and Development

Engaging Question: What valuable insights and experiences did you gain from your first job that still impact you today?

Purpose of this activity:

Understanding the experiences and growth from one's first job can provide valuable insight into the individual's personal and professional development. Additionally, it helps foster a sense of camaraderie and common ground among team members.

Objectives:

- To understand each team member's personal and professional growth journey

- To encourage team members to reflect on and share their experiences from their first job

- To build a sense of common ground and understanding among team members

- To identify transferable skills and lessons learned

from each team member's first job

- To foster a supportive and encouraging team environment

Instructions:

1. Divide the team into smaller groups of 4-5 members each.

2. Each team member is given 10 minutes to reflect on their first job and jot down the lessons they learned that have helped them moving forward in life.

3. After 10 minutes, each team member will take turns sharing their lessons with the group, taking 2-3 minutes each to share.

4. After each team member has shared, the group will have a 10-minute discussion on common themes and insights that emerged from each team member's experiences.

5. Each group will then present their common themes and insights to the larger team, taking 5 minutes for each presentation.

6. The team will then have a 20-minute discussion on how these lessons and experiences can be applied to current and future team projects.

Duration: 1 hour

Materials: Writing paper, pens or pencils

The activity "First Job Lessons" provided an opportunity for team members to reflect on their personal and professional growth journeys and share valuable insights and experiences from their first job. Through group discussions and presentations, common themes and transferable skills were identified, helping to build a sense of common ground and understanding among team members. This activity emphasized the importance of reflecting on our experiences and the impact they have on our personal and professional growth. By sharing our lessons and insights, the team was able to foster a supportive and encouraging environment that will benefit future projects.

BUILDING RELATIONSHIPS: EXPLORING TEAM PERSPECTIVES ON HEALTHY RELATIONSHIPS

Activity 21: Navigating Relationships: Lessons Learned

Engaging Question: What advice have you received in the past that helped you handle a relationship issue, either professional or personal?

Purpose of this activity:

Understanding how team members handle relationships and the advice they have received can foster a supportive environment, where team members can learn from one another and provide advice when needed. It can also help build trust and strengthen relationships within the team.

Objectives:

- To encourage open and honest communication among team members.

- To learn from each other's experiences and challenges in handling relationships.

- To foster a supportive environment within the team.

- To strengthen relationships and build trust among team members.

- To provide opportunities for team members to offer advice and support to one another.

Instructions:

1. Ask the question: "What advice have you received in the past that helped you handle a relationship issue, either professional or personal?" (2 minutes)

2. Give each team member a sticky note and ask them to write down the best advice they received and stick it to the whiteboard (5 minutes)

3. Once everyone has completed the task, ask for volunteers to share their sticky notes and the story behind the advice they received (15 minutes)

4. Encourage team members to ask questions, share their thoughts, and offer support to one another (10 minutes)

5. Use the whiteboard to capture key insights and lessons learned (5 minutes)

Duration: 40-60 minutes

Materials: Whiteboard, markers, and sticky notes.

The activity aimed to encourage open and honest communication among team members, learn from each other's experiences and challenges in handling relationships, foster a supportive environment, strengthen relationships, and build trust. The results of the activity show that team members have valuable experiences and lessons to share, and that working together to support each other can help build a stronger and more cohesive team.

Activity 22: Partnering for Success: Identifying Key Skills

Engaging Question: What are some of the tangible skills or strengths you'd like your work partner to possess to make your projects run more smoothly and efficiently?

Purpose of this activity:

This question helps team members identify areas where they can complement each other's skills and strengths, leading to more successful and productive collaboration.

Objectives:

- To understand the skills and strengths each team member brings to the table

- To identify areas where team members can complement each other to improve project outcomes

- To encourage open and honest communication about work preferences and needs

- To build trust and strengthen partnerships between team members

- To foster a collaborative work environment where everyone feels valued and supported.

Instructions:

1. Divide the team into pairs or small groups (5 minutes)

2. Give each team member a piece of paper and a pen (1 minute)

3. Ask each team member to write down the tangible skills or strengths they would like their work partner to have to make their projects easier (5 minutes)

4. Have each team member share their list with their partner (5 minutes)

5. Encourage open and honest discussion about the lists and why each skill or strength is important (10 minutes)

6. Ask each pair to come up with one or two key skills or strengths that they would like to work on developing together to make their projects run more smoothly and efficiently (15 minutes)

7. At the end of the activity, ask each pair to share their key skills or strengths with the larger group to highlight the diversity of skills and strengths within the team (5 minutes)

Duration: 30-45 minutes

Materials:

➢ Pieces of paper

➢ Pens or markers

This activity helps team members understand each other's skills and strengths and encourages open communication about what each person needs to succeed in their work. By identifying key skills and strengths that they would like to work on together, team members can build stronger partnerships and work more effectively as a team.

Activity 23: Embracing Our Strengths: Exploring the Qualities that Strengthen Relationships

Engaging question: What personal qualities do you possess that you believe have a positive impact on your relationships, both professional and personal?

Purpose of this activity:

This question is important in team building meetings because it allows individuals to reflect on their personal strengths and understand how they can use these strengths to build stronger relationships with others in the workplace. By understanding and appreciating their own qualities, individuals can use this information to better connect with their colleagues and work together more effectively.

Objectives:

- To allow team members to reflect on their personal qualities that enhance relationships

- To promote self-awareness and self-esteem among team members

- To encourage open and honest communication within the team

- To foster a supportive and inclusive workplace environment

- To improve relationships and team dynamics through understanding and appreciation of individual strengths.

Instructions:

1. Start by asking the question: "What personal qualities do you possess that you believe have a positive impact on your relationships, both professional and personal?" (2 minutes)

2. Give each team member 5-7 minutes to reflect and write down their thoughts. (5-7 minutes)

3. Once everyone is finished writing, give each team member an opportunity to share their list with the group. (5-7 minutes)

4. Encourage others to ask questions and provide feedback in a supportive and non-judgmental way. (10-15 minutes)

5. After everyone has shared, have the team discuss the common themes or qualities that were shared and how they can use these qualities to improve their

relationships within the workplace. (20-30 minutes)

6. Conclude the activity by summarizing the key takeaways and how the team can use this information to enhance their relationships and work together more effectively. (5-10 minutes)

Duration: 30-45 minutes

Materials needed: Writing materials (paper, pens/pencils), timer

This activity allowed team members to reflect on their personal strengths and understand how they can use these strengths to enhance their relationships in the workplace. By promoting self-awareness and open communication, this activity helped to foster a supportive and inclusive workplace environment, improving relationships and team dynamics.

Activity 24: Celebrating Our Strengths: Building Better Relationships

Engaging question: What qualities do you admire about yourself that you believe will strengthen your relationships with others?

Purpose of this activity:

This question helps team members reflect on their personal strengths and how they can bring those qualities to their professional and personal relationships. By exploring and appreciating these qualities, team members can develop greater self-awareness and improve their relationships with others.

Objectives:

- Encourage team members to reflect on their personal strengths and qualities

- Foster a supportive and non-judgmental environment for open discussion

- Promote self-awareness and appreciation of personal strengths

- Improve team relationships by encouraging the sharing of qualities and experiences

- Enhance teamwork and collaboration by promoting a deeper understanding of team members.

Instructions:

1. Start by having each team member write down 3-5 qualities they admire about themselves that they believe will enhance their relationships (10 minutes)

2. Next, have each team member take turns sharing their list with the group (30 minutes) Encourage open discussion and reflection by asking follow-up questions such as (20 mins):

3. "How do you think this quality helps you in your relationships?"

4. "Can you give an example of when you have used this quality to build a stronger relationship?" After each team member has shared their list, have the group engage in a discussion about how these qualities can be used to improve relationships within the team (20 minutes)

5. Wrap up the activity by having each team member reflect on one quality they would like to work on in order to further enhance their relationships (10 minutes)

Duration: 60 -90 minutes

Materials:

- Writing materials for each team member
- Whiteboard or flip chart for group discussion

This activity provides a supportive and non-judgmental environment for team members to reflect on their personal strengths and qualities that can enhance their relationships. By sharing and discussing these strengths, team members can build a deeper understanding and appreciation for each other, ultimately leading to stronger relationships and improved teamwork.

EXPLORING TEAM MEMBERS' PERSONALITIES: UNCOVERING WHAT MAKES US UNIQUE

Activity 25: Building our Best Day: A Team-Building Activity

Engaging question: What are some important things you must get done during a day to feel like your best?

Objectives:

- To understand each team member's routines and what helps them feel their best

- To identify common struggles and priorities in the team's daily routines

- To provide support and suggestions for improving personal and team productivity

- To foster communication and collaboration within the team

Instructions:

1. Handout for each team member with the following prompts to fill out with the following prompts and provide time for them to fill out: (15 minutes)

a. Morning time before work: Write down the tasks you like to do that make you feel like your best self

b. Work routines: Write down the tasks you like to do that make you feel like your best self during the day

c. After work routine before bed: Write down the tasks you like to do that make you feel like your best self before bed

d. Highlight the most important tasks for each time frame

e. Write down the tasks you've been struggling to do that you know will make you feel like your best during the day

2. Divide the team into groups of 2-3 people (2 minutes)

3. Each person in the group should fill out the handout with their daily routine and

4. highlight their most important tasks (10 minutes)

5. Each team member will take turns sharing their routine with the group (5 minutes)

6. As a group, discuss the common struggles and priorities, paying attention to the highlighted important tasks (15 minutes)

7. On the whiteboard or poster board, write down the

common struggles and priorities and discuss ways the team can support each other to overcome them (10 minutes)

8. Each team member should suggest one way they could help their partner or the group

Duration: 60 minutes

Materials:

➢ Whiteboard or large poster board and markers

➢ Writing prompts

➢ Small stickers or markers for each team member to highlight their important tasks

This activity allowed team members to understand each other's routines and what helps them feel their best, as well as identify common struggles and priorities in their daily routines. By sharing their routines and important tasks, the team was able to foster communication, collaboration, and provide support to help each other overcome challenges and improve productivity and satisfaction. This activity can be repeated periodically to keep track of changes and progress in routines and to continue building a strong and productive team.

Activity 26: Unleashing Our Superpowers: A Team-Building Activity

Engaging Question: What's one of your personal talents or skills that you consider to be a superpower? How can we utilize these strengths to enhance our team's success?

Purpose of this activity:

Understanding each team member's unique strengths and abilities can help the team work more effectively and efficiently, by allowing each member to contribute in their area of expertise. This activity will encourage team members to reflect on their own skills and to appreciate the strengths of their colleagues, leading to a more cohesive and supportive team.

Objectives:

- To help team members identify their personal strengths and abilities
- To encourage team members to share their skills and talents with the team

- To foster a sense of collaboration and support within the team

- To help the team identify ways to utilize each member's strengths for the benefit of the team

- To improve communication and interpersonal relationships within the team

Instructions:

1. Divide the team into groups of 2-3 people (5 minutes)

2. Hand out a sheet to each team member with the following prompts and have them fill it out (5 minutes):

   A. Write down one of your personal talents or skills that you consider to be a superpower

   B. List 3 ways that this skill could benefit the team

3. Each team member will take turns sharing their personal strength and why they consider it to be a superpower (10 minutes)

4. As a group, discuss how each member's strengths can be utilized for the benefit of the team (15 minutes)

5. On the whiteboard or poster board, write down each team member's strength and label it with their name (5 minutes)

6. Encourage team members to reflect on the activity and discuss any insights or suggestions for how they can utilize each other's strengths in the future (10 minutes)

Duration: 45-60 minutes

Materials:

- Whiteboard or large poster board and markers
- Sticky notes and markers for each team member to post and label their skills on the whiteboard/poster board

This activity allowed team members to understand and appreciate each other's strengths, and to identify ways they can work together to enhance their team's success. By sharing their personal strengths and abilities, the team was able to foster collaboration, support, and a better understanding of each other. This activity can be repeated periodically to keep track of changes and progress in team dynamics and to continue building a strong and cohesive team.

Activity 27: Unwinding and Recharging: Exploring our Ideal Day Off

Engaging Question: What are three things you like to do on your day off to recharge and relax?

Purpose of the activity:

Understanding each team member's preferred method of relaxation and rejuvenation can help build empathy and foster a positive work environment. Team building activities that focus on personal interests and well-being can improve morale and motivation.

Objectives:

- To learn about each team member's preferred method of relaxation and rejuvenation.

- To foster empathy and understanding among team members.

- To improve morale and motivation through a focus on personal interests and well-being.

- To identify common interests and potential team bonding activities.

- To promote open communication and a positive work environment.

Instructions:

1. Introduce the activity and explain the purpose of exploring what activities team members like to do to recharge and relax. (5 minutes)

2. Divide the team into pairs and allocate 7 minutes for each pair to discuss the question "What are three things you like to do on your day off to recharge and relax?" (7 minutes)

3. After 7 minutes, ask each pair to share their conversation with the rest of the team. (5 minutes)

4. As the activities are shared, write them down on the whiteboard or flipchart. (5 minutes)

5. After everyone has shared, take 5 minutes to review the list as a team and see if there are any common activities that many people enjoy. (5 minutes)

6. Using sticky notes, ask each team member to write down the one activity they would like to try or that they haven't done in a while. (3 minutes)

7. Allocate the remaining time for each team member to share why they chose that particular activity. (10 minutes)

Duration: 40 minutes

Materials:

- Whiteboard or flipchart
- Markers
- Sticky notes
- Timer

This activity allowed team members to learn about each other's preferred methods of relaxation and rejuvenation, and to identify common interests and potential team bonding activities. By focusing on personal interests and well-being, the team was able to foster empathy, improve morale and motivation, and promote open communication and a positive work environment. This activity can be repeated periodically to keep track of changes and progress in relaxation habits and to continue building a strong and supportive team.

Activity 28: Unleashing the Alter Ego: Unleash Your Inner Focus

Engaging Question: What would you name your super-focused alter ego and why?

Purpose of this activity:

This question helps to tap into each team member's personal motivation and drive. By exploring their alter egos, team members can better understand what drives them to be productive and focused, which can lead to a more motivated and productive team dynamic.

Objectives:

- To encourage team members to reflect on what drives their focus and productivity

- To allow team members to share their personal motivations with each other

- To promote creativity and imaginative thinking among team members

- To foster a team-building atmosphere of fun and

light-heartedness

- To create a sense of camaraderie and belonging among team members

Instructions:

1. Introduce the activity and explain the purpose of exploring one's super-focused alter ego. Hand out sticky notes and pens to the team. (5 minutes)

2. Ask each team member to take 10 minutes to reflect and answer the question "What would you name your super-focused alter ego and why?" on their sticky notes. (10 minutes)

3. After reflection, ask each team member to share their alter ego's name and why they chose it with the rest of the team. (15 minutes)

4. As each name and explanation is shared, write them down on the whiteboard or flipchart.

5. Allocate 5 minutes for the team to vote on their favorite alter ego name and why it was chosen. (5 minutes)

6. Take 10 minutes to brainstorm as a team on how they can tap into their chosen alter ego during work to increase productivity and focus.

7. Take 5 minutes to wrap up the activity and discuss any insights or observations that emerged.

Duration: 55-60 minutes

Materials needed:

- Whiteboard or flipchart
- Markers
- Sticky notes
- Pens
- Timer

This activity allows team members to tap into their personal motivations and drives, encouraging creative thinking and promoting a fun and light-hearted team dynamic. By exploring each other's alter egos, team members can gain a better understanding of each other and create a stronger sense of camaraderie and belonging.

DISCOVERING YOUR TEAM'S DRIVE: NAVIGATING LIFE AMBITIONS

Activity 28: Sharing Our Triumphs: Reflecting on Personal and Professional Accomplishments

Engaging Question: What personal or professional accomplishment from the past year are you most proud of, and why?

Purpose of this activity:

This question encourages team members to reflect on their individual achievements, fostering a sense of pride and confidence. It also promotes team bonding and open communication by allowing team members to share their experiences and celebrate each other's successes.

Objectives:

- Encourage team members to reflect on their personal and professional accomplishments
- Foster open and honest communication within the team

- Promote a supportive and empowering work environment

- Increase team members' sense of pride and confidence

- Enhance team bonding through shared experiences and discussions.

Instructions:

1. Start by asking the question, "What personal or professional accomplishment from the past year are you most proud of and why?" (5 minutes)

2. Have each team member take turns sharing their accomplishment and explaining why they are proud of it. (15-30 minutes)

3. Encourage other team members to ask questions and offer support and congratulations. (5-10 minutes)

4. To build upon the conversation, ask follow-up questions such as, "What challenges did you overcome to achieve this accomplishment?" and "What did you learn from this experience?" (5-10 minutes)

5. Encourage team members to share their insights and thoughts on the accomplishments shared by others. (5-10 minutes)

6. Conclude the activity by having the team reflect on what they learned about each other and how the shared experiences and accomplishments bring the team together. (5 minutes)

Duration: 45-60 minutes

Materials:

- Whiteboard or flipchart (optional)
- Markers (optional)

This interactive activity allowed team members to reflect on their personal and professional triumphs, promoting open communication and enhancing team bonding. By sharing their accomplishments and engaging in conversations, the team was able to come together and support one another, fostering a supportive and empowering work environment and increasing individual pride and confidence. The activity allowed team members to learn about each other's experiences, strengthening their sense of unity and commitment to their shared goals.

Activity 29: Reflecting on Our Journey: The Past and Future of Our Lives

Engaging question: What did you want your life to look like 10 years ago, and where do you see yourself in the next 10 years?

Purpose of the activity:

Reflecting on personal and professional goals can help team members understand each other's motivations and aspirations, leading to stronger relationships and improved collaboration. Additionally, discussing future goals can help align individual and team goals.

Objectives:

- To encourage team members to reflect on their personal and professional goals

- To provide a space for team members to share their aspirations and motivations

- To foster deeper understanding and empathy among team members

- To align individual and team goals

- To promote open communication and a sense of community among team members

Instructions:

1. Split the team into small groups of 4-5 people. (5 minutes)

2. Each person in the group will have 5 minutes to share their answers to the following prompts (25 minutes):

   a. What did you want your life to look like 10 years ago?

   b. Where are you now compared to that vision?

   c. Where do you see yourself 10 years from now?

   d. What steps do you need to take to get there?

3. After each person has shared, the group can discuss their answers and provide support and encouragement. (20 minutes)

4. Have each group share one key takeaway from their discussion with the larger group. (10 minutes)

Duration: 1 hour

Materials needed:

- Timer
- Whiteboard or flipchart (optional)
- Markers (optional)
- Paper and pen

This activity allows team members to reflect on their personal and professional goals, promoting deeper understanding and empathy among team members, and aligning individual and team goals. By encouraging open communication and a sense of community, the activity strengthens relationships and fosters collaboration.

Activity 30: The Ultimate Choice: Business or Fortune

Engaging Question: Would you rather have the next biggest business idea or win the lottery?

Purpose of this activity:

This question encourages team members to think about their personal values and what they truly value in life. It also helps to foster open and honest communication within the team.

Objectives:

- To encourage team members to think about what they truly value in life.

- To foster open and honest communication within the team.

- To allow team members to share their personal values and beliefs.

- To facilitate discussion and collaboration among team members.

- To challenge team members to think about the pros and cons of each option.

Instructions:

1. Introduction (5 minutes)

   ○ Explain the purpose of the activity and the question that team members will be answering.

2. Writing Reflection (10 minutes)

   ○ Hand out a sheet of paper and pen/pencil to each team member.

   ○ Instruct team members to write down their answer to the question, "Would you rather have the next biggest business idea or win the lottery?" and their reasons why.

3. Small Group Discussion (10 minutes)

   ○ Have team members form small groups of 2-3 people.

   ○ In their small groups, they will discuss their answers and share the reasons why they chose their option.

4. Group Presentation (15 minutes)

- Have each small group present their thoughts to the larger team.

- The larger team can ask questions and provide feedback.

5. Team Discussion (20 minutes)

   - Engage the team in a discussion about the pros and cons of each option and the values and beliefs that led each person to their choice.

   - Write key points from the discussion on the whiteboard or flipchart.

6. Wrap Up (10 minutes)

   - Summarize the key takeaways from the activity.

   - Encourage team members to continue the discussion in future team meetings or one-on-one conversations.

Duration: 60 minutes

Materials:

- Sheet of paper for each team member
- Pen/pencil for each team member
- Whiteboard or flipchart

➢ Markers

This activity encourages team members to think about what they truly value in life and fosters open and honest communication within the team. By breaking into small groups and presenting their thoughts to the larger team, team members are able to share their personal values and engage in discussions about the pros and cons of each option. This activity helps to build trust and understanding among team members and challenges them to think about their priorities and goals in life.

Activity 31: Risk-Taking Rewards: A Team Building Adventure

Engaging Question: What was one of the biggest risks you have taken that has paid off for you now?

Purpose of this activity:

Understanding and reflecting on the risks we have taken and the outcomes they have had can help us better understand what motivates us, what our strengths are, and how we can use these skills to achieve our goals in both our personal and professional lives.

Objectives:

- To encourage team members to reflect on their own risk-taking experiences.

- To provide a space for team members to share their experiences and insights with each other.

- To identify common risk-taking strategies and success factors.

- To encourage team members to think about their own personal and professional goals and how they can use their risk-taking experiences to help achieve these goals.

- To foster collaboration, communication, and trust among team members.

Instructions:

1. Hand out pens and paper to each team member (5 minutes)

2. Give each team member 5 minutes to reflect on their own risk-taking experiences and jot down notes (10 minutes)

3. Have each team member share their story with the group. Encourage everyone to listen actively and ask questions to learn more about each other's experiences (20 minutes)

4. As a group, identify common risk-taking strategies and success factors. Write these on a whiteboard or large piece of paper (15 minutes)

5. Ask each team member to think about their personal and professional goals and how their risk-taking experiences can help them achieve these goals. Write these on a separate sheet of paper (10 minutes)

6. Wrap up the activity by discussing the similarities and differences among team members' goals and risk-taking experiences (10 minutes)

Duration: 70 minutes

Materials:

- Pens and paper for each team member
- whiteboard or large piece of paper for group use

In this team building activity, team members had the opportunity to reflect on their own risk-taking experiences, share these experiences with others, and learn from each other. The group also identified common risk-taking strategies and success factors and discussed how these experiences can be used to help achieve personal and professional goals. This activity helped to foster collaboration, communication, and trust among team members.

Activity 32: Unleashing Personal Growth: Reflecting on the Past 5 Years

Engaging Question: What personal or professional growth have you experienced in the past 5 years that allows you to do something today that you couldn't do before?

Purpose of this activity:

Reflecting on personal and professional growth helps to create a culture of learning and growth within the team. It also allows individuals to see how far they have come and how their experiences have shaped them into who they are today.

Objectives:

- To reflect on personal and professional growth
- To celebrate individual achievements
- To encourage continuous learning and growth
- To foster a supportive and encouraging team culture

- To connect with team members on a personal level

Instructions:

1. Hand out pens and paper to each team member (5 minutes)

2. Write the question on the board or flipchart: "What personal or professional growth have you experienced in the past 5 years that allows you to do something today that you couldn't do before?" (2 minutes)

3. Give each team member 5-7 minutes to reflect and write down their answer on their piece of paper. (5-7 minutes)

4. Once everyone has finished writing, give each team member 2-3 minutes to share their answer with the rest of the team. (2-3 minutes x number of team members)

5. After everyone has shared, allow for 10-15 minutes of discussion, asking the following questions to the whole team to make connections between team members' growth experiences:

    - How has your personal or professional growth impacted the people around you, such as friends, family, or coworkers?

    - What do you see as the next steps in your journey of growth?

6. Finish with a 10-minute wrap-up discussion to celebrate each team member's growth and to reflect on the importance of continuous learning and growth in both personal and professional life.

Duration: 40 - 60 Minutes

Materials Needed:

- Pen/pencil for each team member
- Sheet of paper for each team member
- Whiteboard or flipchart

This activity encourages team members to reflect on their personal and professional growth, celebrate their achievements, and connect with one another on a personal level. It also highlights the importance of continuous learning and growth in both personal and professional life, creating a supportive and encouraging team culture.

Activity 33: CEO for a Day: Who Would You Choose?

Engaging Question: If you had the opportunity to spend a whole day with your favorite CEO, who would it be and what would you like to discuss?

Purpose of this activity:

This question encourages team members to think about their values, aspirations, and professional goals. By discussing the CEOs they admire and what they hope to learn from them, team members can gain insight into their own goals and aspirations and how they align with those of their colleagues.

Objectives:

- To identify the values and qualities that team members admire in their favorite CEOs

- To encourage team members to reflect on their own professional goals and aspirations

- To provide a space for open and honest conversation among team members

- To foster a sense of community and camaraderie among team members

- To help team members understand how they can use the lessons they learn from their favorite CEOs to achieve their own goals.

Instructions:

1. Divide the team into small groups of 4-5 people (5 minutes).

2. Give each group 20 minutes to brainstorm a list of their favorite CEOs (20 minutes).

3. Each group should then select one CEO from their list to focus on for the remainder of the activity (5 minutes).

4. Each group should spend the next 20 minutes preparing a 2-3 minute presentation on why they have selected their chosen CEO and what they hope to learn from spending a day with them (20 minutes).

5. Each group will now give their presentations, allow for open discussion among the teams. Discussion points could include: (15 minutes)

    a. What qualities do they admire in their chosen CEO?

    b. What challenges have they faced in their own careers and how could learning from this CEO help them overcome them?

c. What lessons do they hope to learn from spending a day with their chosen CEO?

   d. How can they apply what they learn to their own professional and personal goals? (15 minutes)

6. Finally, allow 10 minutes for each team to reflect on what they have learned from the activity and what steps they can take to bring their aspirations to life (10 minutes).

Duration: 1 hour

Materials:

- Whiteboard or flipchart
- Markers
- Paper
- Pens

This activity helps team members identify their values and aspirations and how they align with those of their colleagues. By discussing the CEOs they admire and what they hope to learn from them, team members can gain insight into their own goals and what they can do to bring their aspirations to life. This activity helps to foster a sense of community and camaraderie among team members and provides a space for open and honest conversation.

Activity 34: Revelations and Reflections: The Books That Shaped Our Lives

Engaging Question: What's one book that has had a profound impact on your life, and how has it influenced your growth?

Purpose of this activity:

This question encourages team members to think about the books that have had a significant impact on their lives and shaped their perspectives. It provides a chance for team members to reflect on their personal and professional growth and helps build deeper understanding and connection within the team.

Objectives:

- To encourage team members to reflect on their personal and professional growth

- To foster open and honest communication within the team

- To enhance team bonding through shared experiences and discussions

- To provide an opportunity for team members to learn about each other's interests and perspectives

- To encourage team members to share their insights and experiences on the impact of books on their lives

Instructions:

1. Provide sticky notes and pens to each team member.

2. Pose the question, "What's one book that has had a profound impact on your life and how has it influenced your growth?" (5 minutes)

3. Have each team member write down the title of the book on a sticky note and place it on the whiteboard or flip chart. (5 minutes)

4. Have team members group around the books with similar titles and write down their key takeaways and lessons from the book on the flip chart. (10 minutes)

5. If there are individuals who put up books that others haven't read, have them form a group and share their key takeaways and lessons with the rest of the team. (10 minutes)

6. Have each group present their key takeaways, lessons, and how the book has influenced their lives to the whole team. (20 minutes)

7. End the activity by facilitating a discussion on the key

lessons and takeaways the team should begin to use and put into practice for team growth. Write these down on a whiteboard. (10 minutes)

8. Have one of the team leaders send the agreed upon key lessons and takeaways to the whole team and print it out. Have team members place the printout in a visible place in their office to keep each other accountable and support each other's growth. (5 minutes)

Duration: 55 minutes

Materials:

➢ Sticky notes,

➢ Pens

➢ whiteboard or flip chart

➢ printer and paper

This interactive activity allowed team members to reflect on books that have had a profound impact on their lives and provided insight into their personal and professional growth. The activity encouraged open communication, enhanced team bonding, and provided an opportunity for team members to learn about each other's interests and perspectives. By sharing and discussing the insights and lessons from the books, the team was able to identify key takeaways to put into practice for team growth. The team leaders will send these takeaways to the whole team, and team members will keep each other accountable by having the takeaways printed and displayed in their offices.

About The Author:

Dear Team Leaders,

As a trainer of soft skills and conversation coach with more than 11 years of experience, I know how important it is to build a team that is strong, motivated, and works well together. That's why I would like to offer my expertise to help take your team to the next level.

I'm a certified life coach, certified by the Department of Juvenile Justice in Active Listening, Effective Questioning, and Motivational Interviewing, and an ATD certified facilitator and trainer, I bring a wealth of knowledge and experience to the table. I have a proven track record of successfully building and scaling life coaching programs at companies, helping to improve both their bottom line and employee satisfaction.

My approach focuses on helping individuals understand and confront their real feelings, and deal with them in a healthy and effective manner. I believe that this is the missing piece for many people on their journey to peace and fulfillment, and I am dedicated to helping my clients reach that next level.

By working with me as your Conversation Coach, I can help your team members gain a deeper understanding of themselves and each other, leading to improved communication, collaboration, and overall team performance. I offer my latest book as a tool to support your team's growth and development, and I am confident that my expertise will be a valuable asset to your organization.

I look forward to the opportunity to make a positive impact on your team's success.

Sincerely,
Your Conversation Coach, Darius Brown

Additional Resources

"The Best Conversation You Ever Had With Yourself":

Embark on a transformative journey towards self-mastery with "The Best Conversation You Ever Had With Yourself." This book introduces the 4A Process, guiding you to master your inner conversation and unlock a new level of self-awareness, personal growth, and fulfillment. Discover the power of meaningful self-talk and unleash your true potential.

Conversational Anxiety:

Take control of your conversations and overcome anxiety with "Conversational Anxiety." This book provides practical strategies and tools to help you navigate and conquer listening and sharing anxiety. Learn how to establish healthy boundaries, honor your own needs and emotions, and foster connections that feel freeing, connecting, vulnerable, and intentional.

These books, along with other valuable resources, can be found on our website at
www.getyourconversationcoach.com/store.

I believe in the power of continuous learning and personal growth, and these resources will support you in developing effective communication skills and navigating the complexities of conversations.

Visit my website today to explore these books and embark on a journey towards empowering and fulfilling conversations.

Keep In Touch!

We would love to hear from you! If you have any feedback, testimonials, or stories about how this book has impacted your team, please feel free to reach out to us at darius@imdariusbrown.com.

We value your input and appreciate the opportunity to learn more about how this book has made a difference in your team's success. Please share with us any changes you've noticed in your team's key performance indicators (KPIs) from the time you started using this book in your team building meetings until now. Your feedback will help us continue to improve and better serve our readers.

Thank you for your support!

Sincerely,
Your Conversation Coach, Darius Brown

Connect with me on LinkedIn

Made in the USA
Columbia, SC
28 October 2023